AI SOFTWARE BUSINESS

100+ Micro SaaS Ideas To Rapid Launch Your Software Empire

ASIF AHMED

CRESCENT MOON PUBLISHING

ST CLOUD, MN

CONTENTS

Chapter 1:
Explanation of the Concept of Micro SaaS

Are you tired of struggling to come up with a unique business idea? Are you tired of seeing other entrepreneurs hit it big while you are still stuck in the idea development stage?

Look no further because the solution is here - **Micro SaaS!**

In the digital age, Software as a Service (SaaS) has become a dominant force in the software industry, with a vast array of companies utilizing their power to deliver software solutions to customers. However, the recent rise of Micro SaaS has begun to challenge the traditional SaaS model.

Micro SaaS refers to a small, niche-focused software business that operates on a SaaS model.

It is typically a one-person or small team operation that serves a specific market need. It has gained popularity in recent years due to its ability to target underserved markets and provide a more personalized user experience.

Compared to traditional SaaS, Micro SaaS has a lower startup cost and overhead due to its small size and focus on a niche market. This allows for greater flexibility in adjusting and pivoting quickly, as well as the potential for rapid growth and recurring revenue.

One of the primary benefits of Micro SaaS is the ability to target a specific niche market.

By catering to a small segment of customers, Micro SaaS companies can focus on providing highly personalized solutions that are tailored to the unique needs of their target market. This results in a more engaged and loyal customer base that is less likely to churn.

In addition to its niche focus, Micro SaaS also offers flexibility.

Because of its small size and niche focus, a Micro SaaS company can adjust and pivot quickly to changes in the market or to customer needs. This agility allows for a more dynamic and responsive approach to product development and customer service.

Another key benefit of Micro SaaS is the potential for rapid growth and recurring revenue. By serving a specific market need, a Micro SaaS company can achieve a high level of customer loyalty, which can lead to long-term recurring revenue.

Furthermore, the small size of a Micro SaaS company allows it to scale quickly without the need for a large workforce or expensive infrastructure.

Despite the many benefits, there are also potential pitfalls that Micro SaaS companies should avoid.

These include failing to identify a unique value proposition, underestimating the importance of customer acquisition and retention, neglecting the importance of product-market fit, and scaling too quickly without adequate resources and infrastructure.

In order to successfully start a Micro SaaS business, it is essential to follow key steps such as identifying a market need, developing a unique value proposition, establishing a pricing strategy, and creating a marketing plan.

By carefully considering these steps, Micro SaaS companies can build a strong foundation for success in this growing industry.

Chapter 2:
Micro SaaS vs. Traditional SaaS

Software as a Service (SaaS) has been a popular business model for several years now, with many businesses adopting it as a way to deliver software solutions to customers. Traditional SaaS companies tend to be larger organizations that provide a wide range of products and services to a broad customer base. Micro SaaS, on the other hand, is a newer and smaller business model that is focused on serving a niche market.

One of the primary differences between Micro SaaS and traditional SaaS is the size of the companies involved.

Traditional SaaS companies are typically larger organizations with multiple teams and departments, while Micro SaaS companies tend to be smaller, often consisting of just one or a few people.

> *This smaller size can be an advantage for Micro SaaS, as it allows for greater flexibility and agility in responding to customer needs and market changes.*

Another difference between Micro SaaS and traditional SaaS is the focus of the business. Traditional SaaS companies tend to offer a broad range of products and services to a wide customer base, while Micro SaaS companies focus on serving a specific niche market. This narrow focus allows Micro SaaS companies to provide highly tailored solutions that are better suited to the unique needs of their customers.

One of the biggest advantages of Micro SaaS over traditional SaaS is the low startup costs and overhead. Traditional SaaS companies often require significant investment in infrastructure, personnel, and marketing in order to get off the ground. Micro SaaS companies, on the other hand, can be started with very little capital and can operate with lower overhead costs.

This makes Micro SaaS a more accessible option for entrepreneurs and small business owners who may not have access to large amounts of capital.

Another benefit of Micro SaaS is its ability to target niche markets.

Traditional SaaS companies often serve various customers and industries, making it difficult to provide highly specialized solutions. Micro SaaS companies, on the other hand, can focus on serving a specific market segment, allowing them to provide highly tailored solutions that are better suited to the unique needs of their customers.

Finally, Micro SaaS has the potential for rapid growth and recurring revenue. By focusing on serving a specific market need and providing highly tailored solutions, Micro SaaS companies can achieve a high level of customer loyalty, leading to long-term recurring revenue. The smaller size of Micro SaaS companies also allows them to scale quickly without needing a large workforce or expensive infrastructure.

So while traditional SaaS and Micro SaaS share many similarities, there are significant differences that make Micro SaaS an attractive option for entrepreneurs and small business owners. And with the growth of A.I. tools such as ChatGPT access to the market has never been easier or more affordable.

Exciting times for savvy Entrepreneurs like you!

Chapter 3:
Benefits of Micro SaaS

As we've already covered, micro SaaS is a revolutionary business model that offers several benefits to entrepreneurs and small business owners. These benefits include low startup costs and overhead, the ability to target niche markets, the flexibility to adjust and pivot quickly, and the potential for rapid growth and recurring revenue.

One of the primary benefits of Micro SaaS is the low startup costs and overhead. Traditional SaaS companies require significant investment in infrastructure, personnel, and marketing in order to get off the ground...

... Micro SaaS companies, on the other hand, can be started with very little capital and can operate with lower overhead costs. This makes Micro SaaS a more accessible option for entrepreneurs and small business owners who may not have access to large amounts of capital or have a higher level of aversion to risk.

Another benefit of Micro SaaS is its ability to target niche markets. Traditional SaaS companies often serve various customers and industries, making it difficult to provide highly specialized solutions...

... Micro SaaS companies, on the other hand, can focus on serving a specific market segment, allowing them to provide highly tailored solutions that are better suited to the unique needs of their customers. This becomes significant when you begin to factor in things like user churn rates later in the process.

In addition to its niche focus, Micro SaaS also offers flexibility. Because of its small size and niche focus, a Micro SaaS company can adjust and pivot quickly to changes in the market or to customer needs.

This agility allows for a more dynamic and responsive approach to product development and customer service.

Another key benefit of Micro SaaS is the potential for rapid growth and recurring revenue. By serving a specific market need, a Micro SaaS company can achieve a high level of customer loyalty, which can lead to long-term recurring revenue.

Furthermore, the small size of a Micro SaaS company allows it to scale quickly without the need for a large workforce or expensive infrastructure.

Overall, the benefits of Micro SaaS make it an attractive business model for entrepreneurs and small business owners. Its low startup costs and overhead, ability to target niche markets, flexibility to adjust and pivot quickly, and potential for rapid growth and recurring revenue make it an exciting and accessible option for those looking to start their own business.

And by leveraging the benefits of Micro SaaS, almost anyone can build a successful business that delivers value to their customers while achieving long-term financial success for themselves.

Chapter 4:
Pitfalls to Avoid in Micro SaaS

While Micro SaaS offers several benefits, there are also several pitfalls that entrepreneurs and small business owners should be aware of.

These pitfalls include failing to identify a unique value proposition, underestimating the importance of customer acquisition and retention, neglecting the importance of product-market fit, and scaling too quickly without adequate resources and infrastructure.

Probably the most significant of these problems I see often is when the Micro SaaS business fails to identify a unique value proposition.   It can lead to failure before you even get started.

Without a clear and compelling value proposition, it can be challenging to differentiate your business from the competition.

A unique value proposition is what makes your Micro SaaS stand out in the market, and it should be something that resonates with your target customers.   And because this is such a common and critical mistake let's look at this in more detail.

How to Identify a Clear and Compelling Value Proposition for Your Micro SaaS

A unique value proposition is a critical component of any successful Micro SaaS business. It is what sets your business apart from the competition and makes it compelling to your target customers. In this short section, we will explore some tips for identifying a clear and compelling value proposition for your Micro SaaS business (read it twice).

Identify the problem you are solving.

The first step in identifying a clear and compelling value proposition is to identify the problem you are solving for your target customers. By understanding their pain points, challenges, and frustrations, you can develop a solution that addresses their needs and offers a unique value proposition.

Determine your unique selling proposition.

Your unique selling proposition (USP) is what sets your business apart from the competition. It is the unique benefit you offer your customers **that they cannot get from any other business**. Your USP should be a clear and compelling statement that highlights what makes your business unique and why customers should choose you over the competition.

Consider the benefits of your solution.

When developing your value proposition, it is essential to consider the benefits that your solution offers to your target customers. By highlighting the benefits of your solution, you can create a compelling case for why customers should choose your business over the competition. Some benefits to consider might include increased efficiency, reduced costs, improved productivity, or enhanced customer experience.

Gather feedback from potential customers.

To ensure that your value proposition resonates with your target customers, it is essential to gather feedback from potential customers. This feedback can help you refine your value proposition and ensure that it meets the unique needs of your target market. By engaging with your target customers and understanding their needs and pain points, you can create a value proposition that resonates with them and provides a compelling reason to choose your business over the competition.

Focus on the customer experience.

Finally, when developing your value proposition, it is essential to focus on the customer experience. Your value proposition should be centred around how your business can improve the lives of your target customers and enhance their experience.

By focusing on the customer experience, you can create a value proposition that is both <u>compelling</u> and <u>meaningful</u> to your target customers.

By following these tips, you can develop a value proposition that resonates with your target customers, sets your business apart from the competition, and provides a compelling reason to choose your business over the competition.

Okay with that covered let's look at some other mistakes you'll need to be aware of and avoid...

Another critical pitfall to avoid in Micro SaaS is underestimating the importance of customer acquisition and retention.

In a crowded market, acquiring and retaining customers is essential to the success of your business. It is essential to invest in marketing and customer service to attract and retain customers and build long-term relationships with them.

Neglecting the importance of product-market fit is another common pitfall in Micro SaaS. A strong product-market fit is essential for the success of any business, but it is particularly important for Micro SaaS companies that operate in a niche market. To ensure that your product meets the unique needs of your target market, it is essential to conduct extensive market research and gather feedback from potential customers.

Finally, scaling too quickly without adequate resources and infrastructure can be a significant pitfall for Micro SaaS companies. I have seen many promising startups collapse at the point of scaling or when too many users come on board in a short space of time.

While rapid growth is desirable, it is important not to grow too quickly without the proper resources and infrastructure in place. Scaling too quickly can lead to a decrease in product quality, poor customer service, and operational inefficiencies.

For most readers, the benefits of building and operating a Micro SaaS far outweigh any potential issues and pitfalls. Just remember that no matter how exciting an idea is you still need to plan first (do the groundwork) and execute properly in operation. Focus on delivering long-term value to your customers because ultimately that's the fastest route to achieve financial success.

Chapter 5:
Identifying a Market Need for Your Business

One of the most critical steps in starting a successful Micro SaaS business is identifying a market need. Without a clear understanding of the needs and pain points of your target customers, it can be challenging to develop a solution that meets their unique needs and delivers value.

In this chapter, we will explore some tips for identifying a market need for your Micro SaaS business.

Conduct Market Research

The first step in identifying a market need is to conduct market research. This research should include analyzing the industry, researching your competitors, and understanding the demographics and behaviors of your target customers.

- By conducting market research, you can **identify gaps** in the market and determine which customer needs are not being met by the current solutions.

Understand Customer Pain Points

To develop a solution that meets the unique needs of your target customers, it is essential to understand their pain points. This involves understanding the challenges and frustrations that they face in their daily lives and how these pain points impact their work and productivity.

- By understanding their pain points, you can develop a solution that addresses their needs and **provides value**.

Gather Feedback from Potential Customers

Another critical step in identifying a market need is to gather feedback from potential customers. This feedback can be obtained through focus groups, surveys, one-on-one interviews and even analysis by A.I. tools to identify patterns and themes.

- By gathering feedback, you can better understand the needs and pain points of your target customers and develop a solution that meets their unique needs.

Identify Trends in the Market

To identify a market need, it is also essential to identify trends in the market. This includes understanding emerging technologies, changing consumer behaviors, and shifting industry trends.

- By identifying these trends, you can develop a solution that addresses the evolving needs of your target customers and provides **long-term value**.

Consider your Unique Selling Proposition

Finally, when identifying a market need, it is important to consider your unique selling proposition (USP). Your USP is what sets your business apart from the competition and provides a compelling reason for customers to **choose your solution** over the competition.

- By considering your USP, you can develop a solution that addresses a unique market need and provides a compelling value proposition.

Again this is an area a lot of entrepreneurs fail at doing well. And because developing a unique value proposition is a critical step in starting a successful Micro SaaS business we'll dig in here in more detail.

Here are some tips for developing a unique value proposition for your Micro SaaS business.

Identify Your Target Customer

The first step in developing a unique value proposition is identifying your target customer. As we've already covered, this includes understanding their needs, pain points, and behaviors. By understanding your target customer, you can develop a solution that meets their unique needs and provides a compelling value proposition. (this part is critical to your project's long term chances of success)

Understand Your Competition

To develop a unique value proposition, it is also important to understand your competition. Even in the smallest underserved niches you will have competition. So analyze their solutions, understand their strengths and weaknesses, and identify gaps they do not fill. By understanding your competition, you can develop a solution that sets your business apart and provides a compelling reason for customers to choose your solution over the competition.

Determine Your Unique Selling Proposition

Your unique selling proposition (USP) is what sets your business apart from the competition. It is the unique benefit that you offer to your customers that they cannot get from any other business. Your USP should be a clear and compelling statement that highlights what makes your business unique and why customers should choose you over the competition.

Highlight the Benefits of Your Solution

When developing your value proposition, it is essential to consider the benefits that your solution offers to your target customers. By highlighting the benefits of your solution, you can create a compelling case for why customers should choose your business over the competition. Some benefits to consider might include increased efficiency, reduced costs, improved productivity, or enhanced customer experience.

Use Clear and Concise Language

When developing your value proposition, it is important to use clear and concise language that is easy to understand. Avoid using jargon or technical terms that may be confusing to your target customers. Instead, use language that is simple, straightforward, and easy to understand.

Chapter 6:
Establishing a Pricing Strategy for Your Micro SaaS Business

Establishing a pricing strategy is a critical step in starting a successful Micro SaaS business. Your pricing strategy should reflect the value that your solution provides to your target customers and align with your overall business goals.

In this chapter, we will explore some tips for establishing a pricing strategy for your Micro SaaS business.

Determine Your Costs

The first step in establishing a pricing strategy is to determine your costs. This includes calculating the costs associated with developing, maintaining, and delivering your solution. By understanding your costs, you can develop a pricing strategy that ensures that your business is profitable.

Understand Your Target Customer

To develop a pricing strategy that aligns with the needs and behaviors of your target customers, it is important to understand their willingness to pay. This involves understanding the value that your solution provides to your target customers and what they are willing to pay for that value.

Consider Your Unique Selling Proposition

Your unique selling proposition (USP) should also be considered when establishing your pricing strategy. If your solution offers a unique benefit that is not available from other solutions, you may be able to charge a premium price for that benefit.

Analyze the Competition

To develop a pricing strategy that is competitive, it is important to analyze the competition. This involves understanding the pricing strategies of your competitors and identifying gaps in the market. By analyzing the competition, you can develop a pricing strategy that sets your business apart and provides a compelling reason for customers to choose your solution.

Test Your Pricing Strategy

Once you have developed a pricing strategy, it is important to test it with your target customers. This can be done through A/B testing, surveys, or focus groups.

By testing your pricing strategy, you can gather feedback from your target customers and refine your pricing strategy to ensure that it aligns with their needs and behaviors.

With a clear and competitive pricing strategy, you can build a successful Micro SaaS business that delivers value to your customers and achieves financial success.

The next step is equally important...

Chapter 7:
Creating a Marketing Plan for Your Micro SaaS Business

Once you have identified your market need, developed a unique value proposition, and established a pricing strategy, the next step is to create a marketing plan for your new Micro SaaS business.

A marketing plan is a blueprint for how you will promote your business and attract customers so in this chapter, we will explore some key steps to creating a marketing plan for your Micro SaaS business.

Define Your Target Audience

The first step in creating a marketing plan is to define your target audience. Your target audience is the group of people who are most likely to benefit from your solution. By understanding your target audience, you can tailor your marketing efforts to their needs and behaviors.

Determine Your Marketing Channels

Once you have defined your target audience, the next step is to determine the marketing channels that you will use to reach them.

This can include digital marketing channels such as social media, email marketing, and search engine marketing, as well as traditional marketing channels such as print ads and events.

Develop Your Brand Identity

Your brand identity is the visual and verbal representation of your business. This includes your logo, color scheme, messaging, and tone of voice. Developing a strong brand identity can help you stand out from the competition and create a memorable impression on your target audience.

Create Compelling Content

To attract and engage your target audience, you need to create compelling content that showcases the value of your solution.

This can include blog posts, whitepapers, case studies, and videos. Your content should be informative, engaging, and aligned with the needs and behaviors of your target audience.

Measure Your Results

To ensure that your marketing plan is effective, it is important to measure your results. This can include tracking website traffic, social media engagement, and conversion rates. By measuring your results, you can identify what is working well and what needs to be improved.

With a strong marketing plan in place, you can build a successful Micro SaaS business that delivers value to your customers and achieves financial success.

Chapter 8:

Treasure Trove of Micro SaaS Business Ideas

As you have learned so far in this guide, starting a Micro SaaS business can be a lucrative and rewarding venture. By targeting niche markets, staying lean and flexible, and focusing on providing value to your customers, you can create a sustainable source of recurring revenue.

Sometimes just coming up with the ideas themselves can be what keeps people stuck... Not anymore ☺

To help spur your imagination and provide you with a starting point for your own Micro SaaS business, we have compiled a collection of over 100 Micro SaaS business plans.

These plans include SaaS name ideas, tag lines, target audience, and additional data for many kinds of niche markets. From accounting software for freelancers to e-commerce analytics for small businesses, this collection has something for everyone.

What's more, all of these SaaS ideas can be developed using A.I. and with ChatBots created by using tools like ChatGPT and the OpenAI API.

With these powerful tools at your disposal, you can create a scalable and automated Micro SaaS business that delivers value to your customers 24/7.

But the true value of this collection is not just in the individual business plans. It's in the inspiration and creativity that these ideas can spark. As you read through these plans, you may find that they trigger your own ideas and give you the confidence to take the leap and start your own Micro SaaS business.

Imagine the possibilities: a six or seven-figure autopilot income stream that allows you to live life on your own terms, pursue your passions, and make a real impact on the world.

With the right idea and the right execution, it's all within reach.

So dive into this treasure trove of Micro SaaS business ideas, explore the possibilities, and let your imagination run wild. Who knows? Your next big idea could be just a few pages away.

1 ChatPromo: AI-powered Chatbot for Internet Marketers

Alternative Names:

- ChatPromo
- ChatAgent
- ChatGrow

Tagline:

"Automate your marketing with ChatPromo AI chatbot"

ChatPromo is a micro SaaS platform that helps internet marketers to automate their marketing efforts using an AI-powered chatbot. With ChatPromo, you can easily create custom chatbots that can engage with your audience, provide them with valuable content, and convert them into customers.

Target users: Internet Marketers, Small Business Owners

Revenue model: Monthly subscription fee, Freemium model

Marketing Ideas: Guest posts, influencer marketing, and social media campaigns.

2 ChatAffiliate:
Chatbot for Affiliate Marketers

Alternative Names:

- ChatAffiliate
- ChatBoost
- ChatCortex

Tagline:

"Maximize your earnings with ChatAffiliate AI chatbot"

ChatAffiliate is a micro SaaS platform that helps affiliate marketers to increase their earnings with an AI-powered chatbot. With ChatAffiliate, you can easily create custom chatbots that can engage with your audience, recommend products, and provide them with special discounts and promotions.

Target users: Affiliate Marketers, E-commerce Store Owners

Revenue model: Monthly subscription fee, Commission-based model

Marketing Ideas: Email marketing, social media campaigns, and referral programs.

3 ChatEmail:
AI-powered Chatbot for Email Marketing

Alternative Names:

- ChatEmail
- ChatMailer
- ChatMaster

Tagline:

"Revolutionize your email marketing with ChatEmail AI chatbot"

ChatEmail is a micro SaaS platform that helps email marketers to revolutionize their email marketing efforts with an AI-powered chatbot. With ChatEmail, you can easily create custom chatbots that can engage with your subscribers, provide them with personalized recommendations, and increase your email open rates and click-through rates.

Target users: Email Marketers, Content Marketers

Revenue model: Monthly subscription fee, Freemium model

Marketing Ideas: Influencer marketing, content marketing, and social media campaigns.

4 ChatSocial:
Chatbot for Social Media Marketing

Alternative Names:

- ChatSocial
- ChatBoost
- ChatNet

Tagline:

"Transform your social media marketing with ChatSocial AI chatbot"

ChatSocial is a micro SaaS platform that helps social media marketers to transform their social media marketing efforts with an AI-powered chatbot. With ChatSocial, you can easily create custom chatbots that can engage with your followers, provide them with valuable content, and increase your social media engagement and conversions.

Target users: Social Media Marketers, Content Creators

Revenue model: Monthly subscription fee, Commission-based model

Marketing Ideas: Social media campaigns, influencer marketing, and referral programs.

5 ChatAuthor:
Chatbot for Authors and Publishers

Alternative Names:

- ChatAuthor
- ChatBooker
- ChatPublish

Tagline:

"Simplify your publishing journey with ChatAuthor AI chatbot"

ChatAuthor is a micro SaaS platform that helps authors and publishers to simplify their publishing journey with an AI-powered chatbot. With ChatAuthor, you can easily create custom chatbots that can help you with book formatting, publishing, and marketing.

Target users: Authors, Publishers

Revenue model: Monthly subscription fee, Commission-based model

Marketing Ideas: Guest posts, email marketing, and influencer marketing.

6 ChatStore:
Chatbot for E-commerce Stores

Alternative Names:

- ChatStore
- ChatSell
- ChatShop

Tagline:

"Streamline your e-commerce store with ChatStore AI chatbot"

ChatStore is a micro SaaS platform that helps e-commerce store owners to streamline their online store with an AI-powered chatbot. With ChatStore, you can easily create custom chatbots that can engage with your customers, provide them with personalized product recommendations, and increase your e-commerce sales.

Target users: E-commerce Store Owners, Online Retailers

Revenue model: Monthly subscription fee, Commission-based model

Marketing Ideas: Email marketing, content marketing, and referral programs.

7 ChatCreator:
AI-powered Chatbot for Content Creators

Alternative Names:

- ChatCreator
- ChatWriter
- ChatAuthor

Tagline:

"Empower your content creation with ChatCreator AI chatbot"

ChatCreator is a micro SaaS platform that helps content creators to empower their content creation with an AI-powered chatbot. With ChatCreator, you can easily create custom chatbots that can help you with content ideation, creation, and editing.

Target users: Content Creators, Bloggers, YouTubers

Revenue model: Monthly subscription fee, Commission-based model

Marketing Ideas: Influencer marketing, content marketing, and social media campaigns.

8 ChatLink:
AI-powered Chatbot for Link Building

Alternative Names:

- ChatLink
- ChatBack
- ChatRank

Tagline:

"Supercharge your link building with ChatLink AI chatbot"

ChatLink is a micro SaaS platform that helps link builders to supercharge their link building efforts with an AI-powered chatbot. With ChatLink, you can easily create custom chatbots that can help you with link prospecting, outreach, and monitoring.

Target users: Link Builders, SEO Professionals

Revenue model: Monthly subscription fee, Freemium model

Marketing Ideas: Influencer marketing, content marketing, and social media campaigns.

9 ChatLead:
AI-powered Chatbot for Lead Generation

Alternative Names:

- ChatLead
- ChatGenius
- ChatBoost

Tagline:

"Boost your lead generation with ChatLead AI chatbot"

ChatLead is a micro SaaS platform that helps businesses to boost their lead generation efforts with an AI-powered chatbot. With ChatLead, you can easily create custom chatbots that can engage with your prospects, qualify them, and convert them into customers.

Target users: Small Business Owners, Sales Professionals

Revenue model: Monthly subscription fee, Commission-based model

Marketing Ideas: Email marketing, social media campaigns, and referral programs.

10 ChatNews:
AI-powered Chatbot for News Publishers

Alternative Names:

- ChatNews
- ChatRead
- ChatNewsroom

Tagline:

"Deliver personalized news with ChatNews AI chatbot"

ChatNews is a micro SaaS platform that helps news publishers to deliver personalized news to their audience with an AI-powered chatbot. With ChatNews, you can easily create custom chatbots that can curate news articles, send personalized news alerts, and increase your audience engagement.

Target users: News Publishers, Journalists

Revenue model: Monthly subscription fee, Freemium model

Marketing Ideas: Content marketing, influencer marketing, and social media campaigns.

11 ChatScribe:
AI-powered Chatbot for Transcription

Alternative Names:

- ChatScribe
- ChatTranscribe
- ChatDictate

Tagline:

"Transcribe smarter with ChatScribe AI chatbot"

ChatScribe is a micro SaaS platform that helps content creators to transcribe smarter with an AI-powered chatbot. With ChatScribe, you can easily create custom chatbots that can transcribe audio and video content, edit transcriptions, and improve accuracy.

Target users: Content Creators, Podcasters, Video Producers

Revenue model: Monthly subscription fee, Freemium model

Marketing Ideas: Influencer marketing, content marketing, and social media campaigns.

12 ChatInsight: Chatbot for Market Research

Alternative Names:

- ChatInsight
- ChatResearch
- ChatSurvey

Tagline:

"Get valuable insights with ChatInsight AI chatbot"

ChatInsight is a micro SaaS platform that helps businesses to get valuable insights with an AI-powered chatbot. With ChatInsight, you can easily create custom chatbots that can conduct market research, analyze customer feedback, and provide actionable insights.

Target users: Small Business Owners, Market Researchers

Revenue model: Monthly subscription fee, Commission-based model

Marketing Ideas: Email marketing, social media campaigns, and referral programs.

13 ChatCampaign:
AI-powered Chatbot for Ad Campaigns

Alternative Names:

- ChatCampaign
- ChatAd
- ChatBoost

Tagline:

"Optimize your ad campaigns with ChatCampaign AI chatbot"

ChatCampaign is a micro SaaS platform that helps businesses to optimize their ad campaigns with an AI-powered chatbot. With ChatCampaign, you can easily create custom chatbots that can analyze your ad campaigns, suggest optimizations, and improve ROI.

Target users: Digital Marketers, Small Business Owners

Revenue model: Monthly subscription fee, Commission-based model

Marketing Ideas: Email marketing, social media campaigns, and referral programs.

14 ChatEvent:
Chatbot for Event Management

Alternative Names:

- ChatEvent
- ChatPlanner
- ChatOrganizer

Tagline:

"Streamline your event management with ChatEvent AI chatbot"

ChatEvent is a micro SaaS platform that helps event managers to streamline their event management with an AI-powered chatbot. With ChatEvent, you can easily create custom chatbots that can manage event registrations, send event updates, and answer attendee questions.

Target users: Event Managers, Planners

Revenue model: Monthly subscription fee, Freemium model

Marketing Ideas: Influencer marketing, content marketing, and social media campaigns.

15 ChatVirtual: AI-powered Chatbot for Virtual Assistants

Alternative Names:

- ChatVirtual

- ChatAssist

- ChatSecretary

Tagline:

"Simplify your virtual assistant tasks with ChatVirtual AI chatbot"

ChatVirtual is a micro SaaS platform that helps virtual assistants to simplify their tasks with an AI-powered chatbot. With ChatVirtual, you can easily create custom chatbots that can manage your schedule, answer emails, and perform other administrative tasks.

Target users: Virtual Assistants, Freelancers

Revenue model: Monthly subscription fee, Freemium model

Marketing Ideas: Influencer marketing, content marketing, and social media campaigns.

16 ChatSEO:
Chatbot for Search Engine Optimization

Alternative Names:

- ChatSEO
- ChatOptimizer
- ChatRanker

Tagline:

"Optimize your SEO efforts with ChatSEO AI chatbot"

ChatSEO is a micro SaaS platform that helps businesses to optimize their SEO efforts with an AI-powered chatbot. With ChatSEO, you can easily create custom chatbots that can analyze your website, suggest optimizations, and improve your search engine rankings.

Target users: SEO Professionals, Small Business Owners

Revenue model: Monthly subscription fee, Commission-based model

Marketing Ideas: Email marketing, social media campaigns, and referral programs.

17 ChatQuiz:
Chatbot for Quizzes and Surveys

Alternative Names:

- ChatQuiz
- ChatSurvey
- ChatPoll

Tagline:

"Create engaging quizzes and surveys with ChatQuiz AI chatbot"

ChatQuiz is a micro SaaS platform that helps businesses to create engaging quizzes and surveys with an AI-powered chatbot. With ChatQuiz, you can easily create custom chatbots that can engage your audience, collect feedback, and provide valuable insights.

Target users: Digital Marketers, Small Business Owners

Revenue model: Monthly subscription fee, Freemium model

Marketing Ideas: Email marketing, social media campaigns, and referral programs.

18 ChatBrand:
AI-powered Chatbot for Branding

Alternative Names:

- ChatBrand
- ChatDesigner
- ChatLogo

Tagline:

"Create a strong brand identity with ChatBrand AI chatbot"

ChatBrand is a micro SaaS platform that helps businesses to create a strong brand identity with an AI-powered chatbot. With ChatBrand, you can easily create custom chatbots that can design logos, select color schemes, and create marketing materials.

Target users: Small Business Owners, Branding Professionals

Revenue model: Monthly subscription fee, Freemium model

Marketing Ideas: Influencer marketing, content marketing, and social media campaigns.

19 ChatPitch:
AI-powered Chatbot for Elevator Pitch

Alternative Names:

- ChatPitch
- ChatElevate
- ChatPresent

Tagline:

"Craft a perfect elevator pitch with ChatPitch AI chatbot"

ChatPitch is a micro SaaS platform that helps businesses to craft a perfect elevator pitch with an AI-powered chatbot. With ChatPitch, you can easily create custom chatbots that can help you to create an effective pitch, refine it, and practice it.

Target users: Sales Professionals, Small Business Owners

Revenue model: Monthly subscription fee, Commission-based model

Marketing Ideas: Email marketing, social media campaigns, and referral programs.

20 ChatReview: AI-powered Chatbot for Reviews

Alternative Names:

- ChatReview
- ChatRater
- ChatFeedback

Tagline:

"Get more reviews with ChatReview AI chatbot"

ChatReview is a micro SaaS platform that helps businesses to get more reviews with an AI-powered chatbot. With ChatReview, you can easily create custom chatbots that can request feedback, follow up with customers, and increase your online reviews.

Target users: Small Business Owners, Online Retailers

Revenue model: Monthly subscription fee, Commission-based model

Marketing Ideas: Email marketing, social media campaigns, and referral programs.

21 ChatVoice:
AI-powered Chatbot for Voiceover

Alternative Names:

- ChatVoice
- ChatSpeak
- ChatDub

Tagline:

"Get professional voiceovers with ChatVoice AI chatbot"

ChatVoice is a micro SaaS platform that helps businesses to get professional voiceovers with an AI-powered chatbot. With ChatVoice, you can easily create custom chatbots that can generate voiceovers, edit them, and download them in different file formats.

Target users: Content Creators, Marketers

Revenue model: Monthly subscription fee, Freemium model

Marketing Ideas: Influencer marketing, content marketing, and social media campaigns.

22 ChatCrypt:
AI-powered Chatbot for Encryption

Alternative Names:

- ChatCrypt
- ChatSecure
- ChatGuard

Tagline:

"Protect your data with ChatCrypt AI chatbot"

ChatCrypt is a micro SaaS platform that helps businesses to protect their data with an AI-powered chatbot. With ChatCrypt, you can easily create custom chatbots that can encrypt and decrypt data, secure it, and provide you with access control.

Target users: Small Business Owners, Data Privacy Professionals

Revenue model: Monthly subscription fee, Freemium model

Marketing Ideas: Influencer marketing, content marketing, and social media campaigns.

23 ChatEvent: AI-powered Chatbot for Event Management

Alternative Names:

- ChatEvent
- ChatPlanner
- ChatOrganizer

Tagline:

"Streamline your event management with ChatEvent AI chatbot"

ChatEvent is a micro SaaS platform that helps event managers to streamline their event management with an AI-powered chatbot. With ChatEvent, you can easily create custom chatbots that can manage event registrations, send event updates, and answer attendee questions.

Target users: Event Managers, Planners

Revenue model: Monthly subscription fee, Freemium model

Marketing Ideas: Influencer marketing, content marketing, and social media campaigns.

24 ChatTutor:
AI-powered Chatbot for Online Tutoring

Alternative Names:

- ChatTutor
- ChatCoach
- ChatStudy

Tagline:

"Empower your online tutoring with ChatTutor AI chatbot"

ChatTutor is a micro SaaS platform that helps online tutors to empower their tutoring with an AI-powered chatbot. With ChatTutor, you can easily create custom chatbots that can assist in delivering personalized study plans, monitoring progress, and improving learning outcomes.

Target users: Online Tutors, E-learning Platforms

Revenue model: Monthly subscription fee, Freemium model

Marketing Ideas: Influencer marketing, content marketing, and social media campaigns.

25 ChatSmart: AI-powered Chatbot for Smart Homes

Alternative Names:

- ChatSmart
- ChatHome
- ChatHouse

Tagline:

"Control your smart home with ChatSmart AI chatbot"

ChatSmart is a micro SaaS platform that helps people to control their smart homes with an AI-powered chatbot. With ChatSmart, you can easily create custom chatbots that can help you to control your smart home devices, manage schedules, and monitor energy consumption.

Target users: Homeowners, Smart Home Enthusiasts

Revenue model: Monthly subscription fee, Freemium model

Marketing Ideas: Influencer marketing, content marketing, and social media campaigns.

26 ChatCounselor: AI-powered Chatbot for Online Counseling

Alternative Names:

- ChatCounselor
- ChatTherapist
- ChatMentor

Tagline:

"Get support with ChatCounselor AI chatbot"

ChatCounselor is a micro SaaS platform that helps people to get support with online counseling. With ChatCounselor, you can easily create custom chatbots that can provide personalized counseling sessions, monitor progress, and provide feedback.

Target users: Mental Health Professionals, E-healthcare Platforms

Revenue model: Monthly subscription fee, Freemium model

Marketing Ideas: Influencer marketing, content marketing, and social media campaigns.

27 ChatFit:
AI-powered Chatbot for Fitness Coaching

Alternative Names:

- ChatFit
- ChatCoach
- ChatTrain

Tagline:

"Get fit with ChatFit AI chatbot"

ChatFit is a micro SaaS platform that helps people to get fit with an AI-powered chatbot. With ChatFit, you can easily create custom chatbots that can provide personalized fitness plans, monitor progress, and provide feedback.

Target users: Fitness Coaches, Health and Wellness Platforms

Revenue model: Monthly subscription fee, Freemium model

Marketing Ideas: Influencer marketing, content marketing, and social media campaigns.

28 ChatRecruit:
AI-powered Chatbot for Recruitment

Alternative Names:

- ChatRecruit
- ChatHire
- ChatTalent

Tagline:

"Hire smarter with ChatRecruit AI chatbot"

ChatRecruit is a micro SaaS platform that helps businesses to hire smarter with an AI-powered chatbot. With ChatRecruit, you can easily create custom chatbots that can screen job applicants, schedule interviews, and provide insights.

Target users: HR Professionals, Recruitment Agencies

Revenue model: Monthly subscription fee, Commission-based model

Marketing Ideas: Email marketing, social media campaigns, and referral programs.

29 ChatClean: AI-powered Chatbot for Cleaning Services

Alternative Names:

- ChatClean
- ChatMaid
- ChatCleaner

Tagline:

"Clean smarter with ChatClean AI chatbot"

ChatClean is a micro SaaS platform that helps cleaning services to clean smarter with an AI-powered chatbot. With ChatClean, you can easily create custom chatbots that can schedule cleaning appointments, manage customer inquiries, and monitor cleaning services.

Target users: Cleaning Service Providers, Homeowners

Revenue model: Monthly subscription fee, Freemium model

Marketing Ideas: Influencer marketing, content marketing, and social media campaigns.

30 ChatCode: AI-powered Chatbot for Coding Assistance

Alternative Names:

- ChatCode
- ChatDev
- ChatProgram

Tagline:

"Code better with ChatCode AI chatbot"

ChatCode is a micro SaaS platform that helps developers to code better with an AI-powered chatbot. With ChatCode, you can easily create custom chatbots that can assist in debugging, provide code suggestions, and offer personalized programming tips.

Target users: Developers, Coding Bootcamps

Revenue model: Monthly subscription fee, Freemium model

Marketing Ideas: Influencer marketing, content marketing, and social media campaigns.

31 ChatLegal:
AI-powered Chatbot for Legal Assistance

Alternative Names:

- ChatLegal
- ChatLawyer
- ChatLegalEase

Tagline:

"Get legal help with ChatLegal AI chatbot"

ChatLegal is a micro SaaS platform that helps people to get legal assistance with an AI-powered chatbot. With ChatLegal, you can easily create custom chatbots that can provide legal advice, draft documents, and manage legal cases.

Target users: Lawyers, Law Firms, Legal Departments

Revenue model: Monthly subscription fee, Commission-based model

Marketing Ideas: Email marketing, social media campaigns, and referral programs.

32 ChatHealth: AI-powered Chatbot for Healthcare

Alternative Names:

- ChatHealth
- ChatMed
- ChatCare

Tagline:

"Get healthcare support with ChatHealth AI chatbot"

ChatHealth is a micro SaaS platform that helps people to get healthcare support with an AI-powered chatbot. With ChatHealth, you can easily create custom chatbots that can provide personalized medical advice, monitor symptoms, and manage healthcare appointments.

Target users: Healthcare Professionals, E-healthcare Platforms

Revenue model: Monthly subscription fee, Freemium model

Marketing Ideas: Influencer marketing, content marketing, and social media campaigns.

33 ChatInsurance: Chatbot for Insurance Assistance

Alternative Names:

- ChatInsurance
- ChatInsure
- ChatProtect

Tagline:

"Get insurance advice with ChatInsurance AI chatbot"

ChatInsurance is a micro SaaS platform that helps people to get insurance advice with an AI-powered chatbot. With ChatInsurance, you can easily create custom chatbots that can provide insurance advice, compare policies, and manage claims.

Target users: Insurance Brokers, Insurers

Revenue model: Monthly subscription fee, Commission-based model

Marketing Ideas: Email marketing, social media campaigns, and referral programs.

34 ChatRecipe: AI-powered Chatbot for Recipe Suggestions

Alternative Names:

- ChatRecipe
- ChatChef
- ChatCook

Tagline:

"Get recipe suggestions with ChatRecipe AI chatbot"

ChatRecipe is a micro SaaS platform that helps people to get recipe suggestions with an AI-powered chatbot. With ChatRecipe, you can easily create custom chatbots that can suggest recipes based on your preferences, manage grocery lists, and plan meals.

Target users: Food Bloggers, Recipe Sites

Revenue model: Monthly subscription fee, Freemium model

Marketing Ideas: Influencer marketing, content marketing, and social media campaigns.

35 ChatFinance:
Chatbot for Financial Planning

Alternative Names:

- ChatFinance
- ChatMoney
- ChatWealth

Tagline:

"Plan your finances with ChatFinance AI chatbot"

ChatFinance is a micro SaaS platform that helps people to plan their finances with an AI-powered chatbot. With ChatFinance, you can easily create custom chatbots that can provide financial advice, create budgets, and monitor expenses.

Target users: Financial Advisors, Fintech Startups

Revenue model: Monthly subscription fee, Commission-based model

Marketing Ideas: Email marketing, social media campaigns, and referral programs.

36 ChatGardener: AI-powered Chatbot for Gardening

Alternative Names:

- ChatGardener
- ChatGreen
- ChatPlant

Tagline:

"Garden smarter with ChatGardener AI chatbot"

ChatGardener is a micro SaaS platform that helps people to garden smarter with an AI-powered chatbot. With ChatGardener, you can easily create custom chatbots that can provide personalized plant care advice, track plant growth, and manage garden schedules.

Target users: Gardeners, Plant Enthusiasts

Revenue model: Monthly subscription fee, Freemium model

Marketing Ideas: Influencer marketing, content marketing, and social media campaigns.

37 ChatTravel:
AI-powered Chatbot for Travel Planning

Alternative Names:

- ChatTravel
- ChatTour
- ChatWander

Tagline:

"Plan your travel with ChatTravel AI chatbot"

ChatTravel is a micro SaaS platform that helps people to plan their travel with an AI-powered chatbot. With ChatTravel, you can easily create custom chatbots that can provide travel recommendations, book flights and hotels, and manage travel itineraries.

Target users: Travel Agencies, Tour Operators

Revenue model: Monthly subscription fee, Commission-based model

Marketing Ideas: Email marketing, social media campaigns, and referral programs.

38 ChatMusic: AI-powered Chatbot for Music Production

Alternative Names:

- ChatMusic
- ChatBeat
- ChatCompose

Tagline:

"Produce music with ChatMusic AI chatbot"

ChatMusic is a micro SaaS platform that helps people to produce music with an AI-powered chatbot. With ChatMusic, you can easily create custom chatbots that can provide personalized music production advice, suggest sounds, and offer feedback.

Target users: Music Producers, Composers

Revenue model: Monthly subscription fee, Freemium model

Marketing Ideas: Influencer marketing, content marketing, and social media campaigns.

39 ChatTeach: AI-powered Chatbot for Online Teaching

Alternative Names:

- ChatTeach
- ChatEducate
- ChatLearn

Tagline:

"Teach better with ChatTeach AI chatbot"

ChatTeach is a micro SaaS platform that helps online teachers to teach better with an AI-powered chatbot. With ChatTeach, you can easily create custom chatbots that can assist in delivering personalized lesson plans, monitoring progress, and improving learning outcomes.

Target users: Online Teachers, E-learning Platforms

Revenue model: Monthly subscription fee, Freemium model

Marketing Ideas: Influencer marketing, content marketing, and social media campaigns.

40 ChatSales: AI-powered Chatbot for Sales Assistance

Alternative Names:

- ChatSales
- ChatSell
- ChatRevenue

Tagline:

"Boost your sales with ChatSales AI chatbot"

ChatSales is a micro SaaS platform that helps businesses to boost their sales with an AI-powered chatbot. With ChatSales, you can easily create custom chatbots that can assist in lead generation, customer follow-ups, and closing deals.

Target users: Sales Professionals, Small Business Owners

Revenue model: Monthly subscription fee, Commission-based model

Marketing Ideas: Email marketing, social media campaigns, and referral programs.

41 ChatChef: AI-powered Chatbot for Restaurant Menus

Alternative Names:

- ChatChef
- ChatDine
- ChatEat

Tagline:

"Order smarter with ChatChef AI chatbot"

ChatChef is a micro SaaS platform that helps restaurants to order smarter with an AI-powered chatbot. With ChatChef, you can easily create custom chatbots that can provide personalized menu recommendations, manage orders, and monitor food quality.

Target users: Restaurant Owners, Food Service Providers

Revenue model: Monthly subscription fee, Commission-based model

Marketing Ideas: Email marketing, social media campaigns, and referral programs.

42 ChatTraveler: Chatbot for Travel Recommendations

Alternative Names:

- ChatTraveler
- ChatRoam
- ChatAdventures

Tagline:

"Travel smarter with ChatTraveler AI chatbot"

ChatTraveler is a micro SaaS platform that helps people to travel smarter with an AI-powered chatbot. With ChatTraveler, you can easily create custom chatbots that can provide personalized travel recommendations, suggest activities, and offer travel tips.

Target users: Travelers, Travel Bloggers

Revenue model: Monthly subscription fee, Freemium model

Marketing Ideas: Influencer marketing, content marketing, and social media campaigns.

43 ChatFashion:
AI-powered Chatbot for Personal Styling

Alternative Names:

- ChatFashion
- ChatStyle
- ChatTrend

Tagline:

"Style better with ChatFashion AI chatbot"

ChatFashion is a micro SaaS platform that helps people to style better with an AI-powered chatbot. With ChatFashion, you can easily create custom chatbots that can provide personalized fashion recommendations, suggest outfits, and offer style advice.

Target users: Fashion Brands, Stylists

Revenue model: Monthly subscription fee, Commission-based model

Marketing Ideas: Email marketing, social media campaigns, and referral programs.

44 ChatBook:
Chatbot for Book Recommendations

Alternative Names:

- ChatBook
- ChatRead
- ChatLiterary

Tagline:

"Read smarter with ChatBook AI chatbot"

ChatBook is a micro SaaS platform that helps people to read smarter with an AI-powered chatbot. With ChatBook, you can easily create custom chatbots that can provide personalized book recommendations, manage reading lists, and suggest new releases.

Target users: Book Bloggers, Publishers

Revenue model: Monthly subscription fee, Freemium model

Marketing Ideas: Influencer marketing, content marketing, and social media campaigns.

45 ChatFintech: AI-powered Chatbot for Financial Assistance

Alternative Names:

- ChatFintech
- ChatFinanceBot
- ChatMoneyEase

Tagline:

"Simplify finance with ChatFintech AI chatbot"

ChatFintech is a micro SaaS platform that helps people to simplify their finance with an AI-powered chatbot. With ChatFintech, you can easily create custom chatbots that can provide financial advice, create budgets, and monitor expenses.

Target users: Finance Professionals, Financial Institutions

Revenue model: Monthly subscription fee, Commission-based model

Marketing Ideas: Email marketing, social media campaigns, and referral programs.

46 ChatPhotography: AI-powered Chatbot for Photo Editing

Alternative Names:

- ChatPhotography
- ChatEdit
- ChatClick

Tagline:

"Edit photos smarter with ChatPhotography AI chatbot"

ChatPhotography is a micro SaaS platform that helps people to edit photos smarter with an AI-powered chatbot. With ChatPhotography, you can easily create custom chatbots that can provide personalized photo editing advice, suggest filters, and offer feedback.

Target users: Photographers, Photography Enthusiasts

Revenue model: Monthly subscription fee, Freemium model

Marketing Ideas: Influencer marketing, content marketing, and social media campaigns.

47 ChatNews:
Chatbot for News Recommendations

Alternative Names:

- ChatNews
- ChatDigest
- ChatBuzz

Tagline:

"Stay informed with ChatNews AI chatbot"

ChatNews is a micro SaaS platform that helps people to stay informed with an AI-powered chatbot. With ChatNews, you can easily create custom chatbots that can provide personalized news recommendations, manage reading lists, and suggest new sources.

Target users: News Outlets, Media Companies

Revenue model: Monthly subscription fee, Freemium model

Marketing Ideas: Influencer marketing, content marketing, and social media campaigns.

48 ChatGaming: AI-powered Chatbot for Gaming Assistance

Alternative Names:

- ChatGaming

- ChatPlay

- ChatLevelUp

Tagline:

"Play better with ChatGaming AI chatbot"

ChatGaming is a micro SaaS platform that helps people to play better with an AI-powered chatbot. With ChatGaming, you can easily create custom chatbots that can provide personalized gaming advice, suggest games, and offer feedback.

Target users: Gamers, Gaming Studios

Revenue model: Monthly subscription fee, Freemium model

Marketing Ideas: Influencer marketing, content marketing, and social media campaigns.

49 ChatEditor:
AI-powered Chatbot for Blog Editing

Alternative Names:

- ChatEditor
- ChatWrite
- ChatPost

Tagline:

"Edit your blogs better with ChatEditor AI chatbot"

ChatEditor is a micro SaaS platform that helps bloggers to edit their blogs better with an AI-powered chatbot. With ChatEditor, you can easily create custom chatbots that can provide personalized editing advice, suggest content improvements, and offer feedback.

Target users: Bloggers, Content Writers

Revenue model: Monthly subscription fee, Freemium model

Marketing Ideas: Influencer marketing, content marketing, and social media campaigns.

50 ChatTopic:
Chatbot for Blog Topic Suggestions

Alternative Names:

- ChatTopic
- ChatIdeas
- ChatBuzz

Tagline:

"Get blog topic ideas with ChatTopic AI chatbot"

ChatTopic is a micro SaaS platform that helps bloggers to get blog topic ideas with an AI-powered chatbot. With ChatTopic, you can easily create custom chatbots that can provide personalized blog topic suggestions, analyze competitor blogs, and offer trending topics.

Target users: Bloggers, Content Creators

Revenue model: Monthly subscription fee, Freemium model

Marketing Ideas: Influencer marketing, content marketing, and social media campaigns.

51 ChatSEO:
AI-powered Chatbot for Blog SEO Optimization

Alternative Names:

- ChatSEO
- ChatRank
- ChatBoost

Tagline:

"Optimize your blog for SEO with ChatSEO AI chatbot"

ChatSEO is a micro SaaS platform that helps bloggers to optimize their blog for SEO with an AI-powered chatbot. With ChatSEO, you can easily create custom chatbots that can analyze your blog for SEO optimization, provide personalized suggestions, and offer keyword analysis.

Target users: Bloggers, SEO Experts

Revenue model: Monthly subscription fee, Freemium model

Marketing Ideas: Influencer marketing, content marketing, and social media campaigns.

52 ChatSocial:
Chatbot for Social Media Promotion

Alternative Names:

- ChatSocial
- ChatBoost
- ChatPromote

Tagline:

"Promote your blog on social media with ChatSocial AI chatbot"

ChatSocial is a micro SaaS platform that helps bloggers to promote their blog on social media with an AI-powered chatbot. With ChatSocial, you can easily create custom chatbots that can manage your social media accounts, provide personalized content suggestions, and offer social media analytics.

Target users: Bloggers, Social Media Marketers

Revenue model: Monthly subscription fee, Freemium model

Marketing Ideas: Influencer marketing, content marketing, and social media campaigns.

53 ChatMonetize: AI-powered Chatbot for Blog Monetization

Alternative Names:

- ChatMonetize

- ChatRevenue

- ChatCash

Tagline:

"Monetize your blog with ChatMonetize AI chatbot"

ChatMonetize is a micro SaaS platform that helps bloggers to monetize their blog with an AI-powered chatbot. With ChatMonetize, you can easily create custom chatbots that can provide personalized monetization suggestions, analyze revenue streams, and offer financial analytics.

Target users: Bloggers, Content Creators

Revenue model: Monthly subscription fee, Commission-based model

Marketing Ideas: Influencer marketing, content marketing, and social media campaigns.

54 ChatAffiliate: AI-powered Chatbot for Affiliate Marketing

Alternative Names:

- ChatAffiliate
- ChatMarket
- ChatSell

Tagline:

"Sell more with ChatAffiliate AI chatbot"

ChatAffiliate is a micro SaaS platform that helps affiliate marketers to sell more with an AI-powered chatbot. With ChatAffiliate, you can easily create custom chatbots that can assist in lead generation, customer follow-ups, and closing deals.

Target users: Affiliate Marketers, E-commerce Stores

Revenue model: Monthly subscription fee, Commission-based model

Marketing Ideas: Email marketing, social media campaigns, and referral programs.

55 ChatAnalytics: AI-powered Chatbot for Affiliate Analytics

Alternative Names:

- ChatAnalytics
- ChatMetrics
- ChatTrack

Tagline:

"Track your affiliate marketing with ChatAnalytics AI chatbot"

ChatAnalytics is a micro SaaS platform that helps affiliate marketers to track their affiliate marketing with an AI-powered chatbot. With ChatAnalytics, you can easily create custom chatbots that can provide personalized analytics, monitor conversions, and offer affiliate program insights.

Target users: Affiliate Marketers, Affiliate Networks

Revenue model: Monthly subscription fee, Freemium model

Marketing Ideas: Influencer marketing, content marketing, and social media campaigns.

56 ChatNiche:
AI-powered Chatbot for Niche Selection

Alternative Names:

- ChatNiche
- ChatTarget
- ChatAudience

Tagline:

"Find your niche with ChatNiche AI chatbot"

ChatNiche is a micro SaaS platform that helps affiliate marketers to find their niche with an AI-powered chatbot. With ChatNiche, you can easily create custom chatbots that can provide personalized niche suggestions, analyze competitors, and offer trending topics.

Target users: Affiliate Marketers, Digital Marketers

Revenue model: Monthly subscription fee, Freemium model

Marketing Ideas: Influencer marketing, content marketing, and social media campaigns.

57 ChatCampaign: AI-powered Chatbot for Affiliate Campaigns

Alternative Names:

- ChatCampaign
- ChatPromote
- ChatBoost

Tagline:

"Launch better campaigns with ChatCampaign AI chatbot"

ChatCampaign is a micro SaaS platform that helps affiliate marketers to launch better campaigns with an AI-powered chatbot. With ChatCampaign, you can easily create custom chatbots that can manage your campaigns, provide personalized content suggestions, and offer campaign analytics.

Target users: Affiliate Marketers, Digital Marketers

Revenue model: Monthly subscription fee, Freemium model

Marketing Ideas: Influencer marketing, content marketing, and social media campaigns.

58 ChatRevenue: Chatbot for Affiliate Revenue Optimization

Alternative Names:

- ChatRevenue
- ChatMonetize
- ChatBoost

Tagline:

"Optimize your affiliate revenue with ChatRevenue AI chatbot"

ChatRevenue is a micro SaaS platform that helps affiliate marketers to optimize their affiliate revenue with an AI-powered chatbot. With ChatRevenue, you can easily create custom chatbots that can analyze your affiliate programs, provide personalized optimization suggestions, and offer revenue analytics.

Target users: Affiliate Marketers, E-commerce Stores

Revenue model: Monthly subscription fee, Commission-based model

Marketing Ideas: Email marketing, social media campaigns, and referral programs.

59 ChatDesign:
AI-powered Chatbot for Clothing Design

Alternative Names:

- ChatDesign
- ChatCreate
- ChatWear

Tagline:

"Create custom designs with ChatDesign AI chatbot"

ChatDesign is a micro SaaS platform that helps print on demand clothing sellers to create custom designs with an AI-powered chatbot. With ChatDesign, you can easily create custom chatbots that can assist in designing custom clothing, provide suggestions for design elements, and offer feedback.

Target users: Print on Demand Clothing Sellers, Fashion Designers

Revenue model: Monthly subscription fee, Commission-based model

Marketing Ideas: Email marketing, social media campaigns, and referral programs.

60 ChatStore:
Chatbot for Clothing Store Management

Alternative Names:

- ChatStore
- ChatManage
- ChatSell

Tagline:

"Manage your clothing store better with ChatStore AI chatbot"

ChatStore is a micro SaaS platform that helps print on demand clothing sellers to manage their clothing store better with an AI-powered chatbot. With ChatStore, you can easily create custom chatbots that can assist in managing clothing inventory, processing orders, and managing customer support.

Target users: Print on Demand Clothing Sellers, E-commerce Stores

Revenue model: Monthly subscription fee, Commission-based model

Marketing Ideas: Email marketing, social media campaigns, and referral programs.

61 ChatMarketing: AI-powered Chatbot for Clothing Marketing

Alternative Names:

- ChatMarketing
- ChatPromote
- ChatBoost

Tagline:

"Promote your clothing with ChatMarketing AI chatbot"

ChatMarketing is a micro SaaS platform that helps print on demand clothing sellers to promote their clothing with an AI-powered chatbot. With ChatMarketing, you can easily create custom chatbots that can manage your social media accounts, provide personalized content suggestions, and offer social media analytics.

Target users: Print on Demand Clothing Sellers, Digital Marketers

Revenue model: Monthly subscription fee, Commission-based model

Marketing Ideas: Email marketing, social media campaigns, and referral programs.

62 ChatAnalytics:
Chatbot for Clothing Sales Analytics

Alternative Names:

- ChatAnalytics
- ChatMetrics
- ChatTrack

Tagline:

"Track your clothing sales with ChatAnalytics AI chatbot"

ChatAnalytics is a micro SaaS platform that helps print on demand clothing sellers to track their clothing sales with an AI-powered chatbot. With ChatAnalytics, you can easily create custom chatbots that can provide personalized analytics, monitor sales, and offer customer insights.

Target users: Print on Demand Clothing Sellers, E-commerce Stores

Revenue model: Monthly subscription fee, Freemium model

Marketing Ideas: Influencer marketing, content marketing, and social media campaigns.

63 ChatRevenue: Chatbot for Clothing Revenue Optimization

Alternative Names:

- ChatRevenue
- ChatMonetize
- ChatBoost

Tagline:

"Optimize your clothing revenue with ChatRevenue AI chatbot"

ChatRevenue is a micro SaaS platform that helps print on demand clothing sellers to optimize their clothing revenue with an AI-powered chatbot. With ChatRevenue, you can easily create custom chatbots that can analyze your sales data, provide personalized optimization suggestions, and offer revenue analytics.

Target users: Print on Demand Clothing Sellers, E-commerce Stores

Revenue model: Monthly subscription fee, Commission-based model

Marketing Ideas: Email marketing, social media campaigns, and referral programs.

64 ChatList:
Chatbot for Email List Management

Alternative Names:

- ChatList
- ChatManage
- ChatGrow

Tagline:

"Manage and grow your email list with ChatList AI chatbot"

ChatList is a micro SaaS platform that helps email marketers to manage and grow their email list with an AI-powered chatbot. With ChatList, you can easily create custom chatbots that can assist in managing email lists, segmenting subscribers, and provide suggestions for increasing subscribers.

Target users: Email Marketers, Digital Marketers

Revenue model: Monthly subscription fee, Freemium model

Marketing Ideas: Influencer marketing, content marketing, and social media campaigns.

65 ChatCampaign: AI-powered Chatbot for Email Campaigns

Alternative Names:

- ChatCampaign
- ChatPromote
- ChatBoost

Tagline:

"Launch better email campaigns with ChatCampaign AI chatbot"

ChatCampaign is a micro SaaS platform that helps email marketers to launch better email campaigns with an AI-powered chatbot. With ChatCampaign, you can easily create custom chatbots that can manage your email campaigns, provide personalized content suggestions, and offer campaign analytics.

Target users: Email Marketers, Digital Marketers

Revenue model: Monthly subscription fee, Freemium model

Marketing Ideas: Influencer marketing, content marketing, and social media campaigns.

66 ChatOptimize: AI-powered Chatbot for Email Optimization

Alternative Names:

- ChatOptimize
- ChatBoost
- ChatMonetize

Tagline:

"Optimize your email marketing with ChatOptimize AI chatbot"

ChatOptimize is a micro SaaS platform that helps email marketers to optimize their email marketing with an AI-powered chatbot. With ChatOptimize, you can easily create custom chatbots that can analyze your email campaigns, provide personalized optimization suggestions, and offer revenue analytics.

Target users: Email Marketers, Digital Marketers

Revenue model: Monthly subscription fee, Commission-based model

Marketing Ideas: Influencer marketing, content marketing, and social media campaigns.

67 ChatCopywriting: AI-powered Chatbot for Email Copywriting

Alternative Names:

- ChatCopywriting
- ChatWrite
- ChatCopy

Tagline:

"Write better email copy with ChatCopywriting AI chatbot"

ChatCopywriting is a micro SaaS platform that helps email marketers to write better email copy with an AI-powered chatbot. With ChatCopywriting, you can easily create custom chatbots that can provide personalized copywriting advice, suggest content improvements, and offer feedback.

Target users: Email Marketers, Digital Marketers

Revenue model: Monthly subscription fee, Freemium model

Marketing Ideas: Influencer marketing, content marketing, and social media campaigns.

68 ChatAnalytics:
AI-powered Chatbot for Email Analytics

Alternative Names:

- ChatAnalytics
- ChatMetrics
- ChatTrack

Tagline:

"Track your email marketing with ChatAnalytics AI chatbot"

ChatAnalytics is a micro SaaS platform that helps email marketers to track their email marketing with an AI-powered chatbot. With ChatAnalytics, you can easily create custom chatbots that can provide personalized analytics, monitor conversions, and offer email marketing insights.

Target users: Email Marketers, Digital Marketers

Revenue model: Monthly subscription fee, Freemium model

Marketing Ideas: Influencer marketing, content marketing, and social media campaigns.

69 ChatSchedule:
Chatbot for Fitness Class Scheduling

Alternative Names:

- ChatSchedule
- ChatBook
- ChatFit

Tagline:

"Schedule your fitness classes with ChatSchedule AI chatbot"

ChatSchedule is a micro SaaS platform that helps fitness instructors to schedule their fitness classes with an AI-powered chatbot. With ChatSchedule, you can easily create custom chatbots that can assist in class scheduling, class bookings, and client reminders.

Target users: Health and Fitness Instructors, Fitness Studios

Revenue model: Monthly subscription fee, Commission-based model

Marketing Ideas: Email marketing, social media campaigns, and referral programs.

70 ChatWorkout: AI-powered Chatbot for Fitness Workouts

Alternative Names:

- ChatWorkout
- ChatFit
- ChatMove

Tagline:

"Get personalized fitness workouts with ChatWorkout AI chatbot"

ChatWorkout is a micro SaaS platform that helps fitness instructors to provide personalized fitness workouts with an AI-powered chatbot. With ChatWorkout, you can easily create custom chatbots that can provide personalized fitness workouts, offer nutrition advice, and monitor fitness progress.

Target users: Health and Fitness Instructors, Personal Trainers

Revenue model: Monthly subscription fee, Commission-based model

Marketing Ideas: Email marketing, social media campaigns, and referral programs.

71 ChatNutrition:
AI-powered Chatbot for Fitness Nutrition

Alternative Names:

- ChatNutrition
- ChatFood
- ChatFuel

Tagline:

"Get personalized nutrition advice with ChatNutrition AI chatbot"

ChatNutrition is a micro SaaS platform that helps fitness instructors to provide personalized nutrition advice with an AI-powered chatbot. With ChatNutrition, you can easily create custom chatbots that can provide personalized nutrition plans, offer meal suggestions, and monitor diet progress.

Target users: Health and Fitness Instructors, Nutritionists

Revenue model: Monthly subscription fee, Commission-based model

Marketing Ideas: Email marketing, social media campaigns, and referral programs.

72 ChatCommunity:
Chatbot for Fitness Community Building

Alternative Names:

- ChatCommunity
- ChatConnect
- ChatGather

Tagline:

"Build your fitness community with ChatCommunity AI chatbot"

ChatCommunity is a micro SaaS platform that helps fitness instructors to build their fitness community with an AI-powered chatbot. With ChatCommunity, you can easily create custom chatbots that can manage community engagement, provide personalized feedback, and offer community analytics.

Target users: Health and Fitness Instructors, Fitness Studios

Revenue model: Monthly subscription fee, Freemium model

Marketing Ideas: Influencer marketing, content marketing, and social media campaigns.

73 ChatAnalytics:
AI-powered Chatbot for Fitness Analytics

Alternative Names:

- ChatAnalytics
- ChatMetrics
- ChatTrack

Tagline:

"Track your fitness progress with ChatAnalytics AI chatbot"

ChatAnalytics is a micro SaaS platform that helps fitness instructors to track their fitness progress with an AI-powered chatbot. With ChatAnalytics, you can easily create custom chatbots that can provide personalized analytics, monitor fitness progress, and offer client insights.

Target users: Health and Fitness Instructors, Personal Trainers

Revenue model: Monthly subscription fee, Freemium model

Marketing Ideas: Influencer marketing, content marketing, and social media campaigns.

74 ChatEd:
Chatbot for Health and Wellness Education

Alternative Names:

- ChatEd
- ChatLearn
- ChatEducate

Tagline:

"Learn about health and wellness with ChatEd AI chatbot"

ChatEd is a micro SaaS platform that helps health and wellness educators to educate their audience with an AI-powered chatbot. With ChatEd, you can easily create custom chatbots that can provide personalized health and wellness information, offer educational resources, and answer questions.

Target users: Health and Wellness Educators, Health Coaches

Revenue model: Monthly subscription fee, Commission-based model

Marketing Ideas: Email marketing, social media campaigns, and referral programs.

75 ChatNutrition: AI-powered Chatbot for Nutrition Education

Alternative Names:

- ChatNutrition
- ChatFood
- ChatFuel

Tagline:

"Learn about nutrition with ChatNutrition AI chatbot"

ChatNutrition is a micro SaaS platform that helps health and wellness educators to educate their audience about nutrition with an AI-powered chatbot. With ChatNutrition, you can easily create custom chatbots that can provide personalized nutrition information, offer healthy recipes, and answer questions.

Target users: Health and Wellness Educators, Nutritionists

Revenue model: Monthly subscription fee, Commission-based model

Marketing Ideas: Email marketing, social media campaigns, and referral programs.

76 ChatMental:
Chatbot for Mental Health Education

Alternative Names:

- ChatMental
- ChatMind
- ChatTherapy

Tagline:

"Learn about mental health with ChatMental AI chatbot"

ChatMental is a micro SaaS platform that helps health and wellness educators to educate their audience about mental health with an AI-powered chatbot. With ChatMental, you can easily create custom chatbots that can provide personalized mental health information, offer self-care resources, and answer questions.

Target users: Health and Wellness Educators, Mental Health Professionals

Revenue model: Monthly subscription fee, Commission-based model

Marketing Ideas: Email marketing, social media campaigns, and referral programs.

77 ChatCommunity:
Chatbot for Health/Wellness Building

Alternative Names:

- ChatCommunity
- ChatConnect
- ChatGather

Tagline:

"Build your health and wellness community with ChatCommunity AI chatbot"

ChatCommunity is a micro SaaS platform that helps health and wellness educators to build their community with an AI-powered chatbot. With ChatCommunity, you can easily create custom chatbots that can manage community engagement, provide personalized feedback, and offer community analytics.

Target users: Health and Wellness Educators, Health Coaches

Revenue model: Monthly subscription fee, Freemium model

Marketing Ideas: Influencer marketing, content marketing, and social media campaigns.

78 ChatAnalytics:
Chatbot for Health and Wellness
Analytics

Alternative Names:

- ChatAnalytics
- ChatMetrics
- ChatTrack

Tagline:

"Track your health and wellness progress with ChatAnalytics AI chatbot"

ChatAnalytics is a micro SaaS platform that helps health and wellness educators to track their progress with an AI-powered chatbot. With ChatAnalytics, you can easily create custom chatbots that can provide personalized analytics, monitor progress, and offer insights.

Target users: Health and Wellness Educators, Health Coaches

Revenue model: Monthly subscription fee, Freemium model

Marketing Ideas: Influencer marketing, content marketing, and social media campaigns.

79 ChatDesign: AI-powered Chatbot for SaaS Design

Alternative Names:

- ChatDesign
- ChatCreate
- ChatBuild

Tagline:

"Create better SaaS designs with ChatDesign AI chatbot"

ChatDesign is a micro SaaS platform that helps SaaS builders to create better designs with an AI-powered chatbot. With ChatDesign, you can easily create custom chatbots that can assist in designing SaaS interfaces, provide suggestions for design elements, and offer feedback.

Target users: SaaS Builders, UX Designers

Revenue model: Monthly subscription fee, Commission-based model

Marketing Ideas: Email marketing, social media campaigns, and referral programs.

80 ChatDevelopment: AI-powered Chatbot for SaaS Development

Alternative Names:

- ChatDevelopment
- ChatBuild
- ChatCode

Tagline:

"Develop better SaaS products with ChatDevelopment AI chatbot"

ChatDevelopment is a micro SaaS platform that helps SaaS builders to develop better products with an AI-powered chatbot. With ChatDevelopment, you can easily create custom chatbots that can assist in SaaS development, provide suggestions for coding best practices, and offer feedback.

Target users: SaaS Builders, Software Developers

Revenue model: Monthly subscription fee, Commission-based model

Marketing Ideas: Email marketing, social media campaigns, and referral programs.

81 ChatMarketing:
AI-powered Chatbot for SaaS Marketing

Alternative Names:

- ChatMarketing
- ChatPromote
- ChatBoost

Tagline:

"Promote your SaaS product with ChatMarketing AI chatbot"

ChatMarketing is a micro SaaS platform that helps SaaS builders to promote their products with an AI-powered chatbot. With ChatMarketing, you can easily create custom chatbots that can manage your social media accounts, provide personalized content suggestions, and offer social media analytics.

Target users: SaaS Builders, Digital Marketers

Revenue model: Monthly subscription fee, Commission-based model

Marketing Ideas: Email marketing, social media campaigns, and referral programs.

82 ChatAnalytics:
AI-powered Chatbot for SaaS Analytics

Alternative Names:

- ChatAnalytics
- ChatMetrics
- ChatTrack

Tagline:

"Track your SaaS product with ChatAnalytics AI chatbot"

ChatAnalytics is a micro SaaS platform that helps SaaS builders to track their products with an AI-powered chatbot. With ChatAnalytics, you can easily create custom chatbots that can provide personalized analytics, monitor conversions, and offer product insights.

Target users: SaaS Builders, Digital Marketers

Revenue model: Monthly subscription fee, Freemium model

Marketing Ideas: Influencer marketing, content marketing, and social media campaigns.

83 ChatRevenue:
Chatbot for SaaS Revenue Optimization

Alternative Names:

- ChatRevenue
- ChatMonetize
- ChatBoost

Tagline:

"Optimize your SaaS revenue with ChatRevenue AI chatbot"

ChatRevenue is a micro SaaS platform that helps SaaS builders to optimize their revenue with an AI-powered chatbot. With ChatRevenue, you can easily create custom chatbots that can analyze your sales data, provide personalized optimization suggestions, and offer revenue analytics.

Target users: SaaS Builders, Digital Marketers

Revenue model: Monthly subscription fee, Commission-based model

Marketing Ideas: Email marketing, social media campaigns, and referral programs.

84 ChatCyber:
Cybersecurity Assistance

Alternative Names:

- ChatCyber
- ChatSecure
- ChatProtect

Tagline:

"Get assistance in cybersecurity with ChatCyber AI chatbot"

ChatCyber is a micro SaaS platform that helps cybersecurity experts to provide assistance to clients with an AI-powered chatbot. With ChatCyber, you can easily create custom chatbots that can assist in cybersecurity planning, provide tips for data protection, and offer incident response strategies.

Target users: Cybersecurity Experts, IT Professionals

Revenue model: Monthly subscription fee, Commission-based model

Marketing Ideas: Email marketing, social media campaigns, and referral programs.

85 ChatCompliance: Cybersecurity Compliance

Alternative Names:

- ChatCompliance
- ChatSecure
- ChatRegulate

Tagline:

"Achieve compliance in cybersecurity with ChatCompliance AI chatbot"

ChatCompliance is a micro SaaS platform that helps cybersecurity experts to achieve compliance with an AI-powered chatbot. With ChatCompliance, you can easily create custom chatbots that can assist in compliance planning, provide industry-specific compliance regulations, and offer audit support.

Target users: Cybersecurity Experts, IT Professionals

Revenue model: Monthly subscription fee, Commission-based model

Marketing Ideas: Email marketing, social media campaigns, and referral programs.

86 ChatIncident: Cybersecurity Incident Management

Alternative Names:

- ChatIncident
- ChatResponse
- ChatRecover

Tagline:

"Manage cybersecurity incidents with ChatIncident AI chatbot"

ChatIncident is a micro SaaS platform that helps cybersecurity experts to manage incidents with an AI-powered chatbot. With ChatIncident, you can easily create custom chatbots that can assist in incident management, provide response strategies, and offer forensic support.

Target users: Cybersecurity Experts, IT Professionals

Revenue model: Monthly subscription fee, Commission-based model

Marketing Ideas: Email marketing, social media campaigns, and referral programs.

87 ChatTraining: AI-powered Chatbot for Cybersecurity Training

Alternative Names:

- ChatTraining
- ChatEducate
- ChatLearn

Tagline:

"Train in cybersecurity with ChatTraining AI chatbot"

ChatTraining is a micro SaaS platform that helps cybersecurity experts to train their clients with an AI-powered chatbot. With ChatTraining, you can easily create custom chatbots that can provide personalized training content, offer industry-specific certifications, and monitor client progress.

Target users: Cybersecurity Experts, IT Professionals

Revenue model: Monthly subscription fee, Commission-based model

Marketing Ideas: Email marketing, social media campaigns, and referral programs.

88 ChatAnalytics:
Chatbot for Cybersecurity Analytics

Alternative Names:

- ChatAnalytics
- ChatMetrics
- ChatTrack

Tagline:

"Track your cybersecurity with ChatAnalytics AI chatbot"

ChatAnalytics is a micro SaaS platform that helps cybersecurity experts to track their cybersecurity with an AI-powered chatbot. With ChatAnalytics, you can easily create custom chatbots that can provide personalized analytics, monitor cybersecurity progress, and offer client insights.

Target users: Cybersecurity Experts, IT Professionals

Revenue model: Monthly subscription fee, Freemium model

Marketing Ideas: Influencer marketing, content marketing, and social media campaigns.

89 ChatAI:
AI-powered Chatbot for AI Assistance

Alternative Names:

- ChatAI
- ChatAssist
- ChatExpert

Tagline:

"Get assistance in AI with ChatAI AI chatbot"

ChatAI is a micro SaaS platform that helps AI experts and prompt engineers to provide assistance to clients with an AI-powered chatbot. With ChatAI, you can easily create custom chatbots that can assist in AI modeling, provide training resources, and offer insights.

Target users: AI Experts, Prompt Engineers

Revenue model: Monthly subscription fee, Commission-based model

Marketing Ideas: Email marketing, social media campaigns, and referral programs.

90 ChatGeneration: AI-powered Chatbot for Prompt Generation

Alternative Names:

- ChatGeneration
- ChatPrompt
- ChatCreate

Tagline:

"Generate better prompts with ChatGeneration AI chatbot"

ChatGeneration is a micro SaaS platform that helps AI experts and prompt engineers to generate better prompts with an AI-powered chatbot. With ChatGeneration, you can easily create custom chatbots that can assist in prompt generation, provide training resources, and offer feedback.

Target users: AI Experts, Prompt Engineers

Revenue model: Monthly subscription fee, Commission-based model

Marketing Ideas: Email marketing, social media campaigns, and referral programs.

91 ChatDevelopment: AI-powered Chatbot for AI Development

Alternative Names:

- ChatDevelopment
- ChatBuild
- ChatCode

Tagline:

"Develop better AI products with ChatDevelopment AI chatbot"

ChatDevelopment is a micro SaaS platform that helps AI experts and prompt engineers to develop better products with an AI-powered chatbot. With ChatDevelopment, you can easily create custom chatbots that can assist in AI development, provide suggestions for coding best practices, and offer feedback.

Target users: AI Experts, Prompt Engineers

Revenue model: Monthly subscription fee, Commission-based model

Marketing Ideas: Email marketing, social media campaigns, and referral programs.

92 ChatTesting:
AI-powered Chatbot for AI Testing

Alternative Names:

- ChatTesting
- ChatTest
- ChatVerify

Tagline:

"Test your AI products with ChatTesting AI chatbot"

ChatTesting is a micro SaaS platform that helps AI experts and prompt engineers to test their products with an AI-powered chatbot. With ChatTesting, you can easily create custom chatbots that can assist in AI testing, provide suggestions for performance improvements, and offer feedback.

Target users: AI Experts, Prompt Engineers

Revenue model: Monthly subscription fee, Commission-based model

Marketing Ideas: Email marketing, social media campaigns, and referral programs.

93 ChatAnalytics:
AI-powered Chatbot for AI Analytics

Alternative Names:

- ChatAnalytics
- ChatMetrics
- ChatTrack

Tagline:

"Track your AI progress with ChatAnalytics AI chatbot"

ChatAnalytics is a micro SaaS platform that helps AI experts and prompt engineers to track their progress with an AI-powered chatbot. With ChatAnalytics, you can easily create custom chatbots that can provide personalized analytics, monitor AI progress, and offer insights.

Target users: AI Experts, Prompt Engineers

Revenue model: Monthly subscription fee, Freemium model

Marketing Ideas: Influencer marketing, content marketing, and social media campaigns.

94 ChatVideo:
AI-powered Chatbot for Video Editing

Alternative Names:

- ChatVideo
- ChatEdit
- ChatCreate

Tagline:

"Edit better videos with ChatVideo AI chatbot"

ChatVideo is a micro SaaS platform that helps YouTubers to edit better videos with an AI-powered chatbot. With ChatVideo, you can easily create custom chatbots that can assist in video editing, provide suggestions for video optimization, and offer feedback.

Target users: YouTubers, Video Editors

Revenue model: Monthly subscription fee, Commission-based model

Marketing Ideas: Email marketing, social media campaigns, and referral programs.

95 ChatSEO:
AI-powered Chatbot for YouTube SEO

Alternative Names:

- ChatSEO
- ChatOptimize
- ChatRank

Tagline:

"Rank better on YouTube with ChatSEO AI chatbot"

ChatSEO is a micro SaaS platform that helps YouTubers to rank better on YouTube with an AI-powered chatbot. With ChatSEO, you can easily create custom chatbots that can assist in YouTube SEO, provide suggestions for video optimization, and offer analytics.

Target users: YouTubers, Digital Marketers

Revenue model: Monthly subscription fee, Commission-based model

Marketing Ideas: Email marketing, social media campaigns, and referral programs.

96 ChatEngage:
Chatbot for YouTube Engagement

Alternative Names:

- ChatEngage
- ChatAudience
- ChatConnect

Tagline:

"Engage better with your YouTube audience with ChatEngage AI chatbot"

ChatEngage is a micro SaaS platform that helps YouTubers to engage better with their audience with an AI-powered chatbot. With ChatEngage, you can easily create custom chatbots that can manage your social media accounts, provide personalized content suggestions, and offer audience analytics.

Target users: YouTubers, Social Media Managers

Revenue model: Monthly subscription fee, Commission-based model

Marketing Ideas: Email marketing, social media campaigns, and referral programs.

97 ChatPromotion: AI-powered Chatbot for YouTube Promotion

Alternative Names:

- ChatPromotion
- ChatBoost
- ChatGrow

Tagline:

"Promote your YouTube channel with ChatPromotion AI chatbot"

ChatPromotion is a micro SaaS platform that helps YouTubers to promote their channels with an AI-powered chatbot. With ChatPromotion, you can easily create custom chatbots that can manage your social media accounts, provide personalized promotion suggestions, and offer analytics.

Target users: YouTubers, Digital Marketers

Revenue model: Monthly subscription fee, Commission-based model

Marketing Ideas: Email marketing, social media campaigns, and referral programs.

98 ChatAnalytics: AI-powered Chatbot for YouTube Analytics

Alternative Names:

- ChatAnalytics
- ChatMetrics
- ChatTrack

Tagline:

"Track your YouTube progress with ChatAnalytics AI chatbot"

ChatAnalytics is a micro SaaS platform that helps YouTubers to track their progress with an AI-powered chatbot. With ChatAnalytics, you can easily create custom chatbots that can provide personalized analytics, monitor YouTube progress, and offer insights.

Target users: YouTubers, Digital Marketers

Revenue model: Monthly subscription fee, Freemium model

Marketing Ideas: Influencer marketing, content marketing, and social media campaigns.

99 ChatVideo: Chatbot for TikTok Video Editing

Alternative Names:

- ChatVideo
- ChatEdit
- ChatCreate

Tagline:

"Edit better TikTok videos with ChatVideo AI chatbot"

ChatVideo is a micro SaaS platform that helps TikTokers to edit better videos with an AI-powered chatbot. With ChatVideo, you can easily create custom chatbots that can assist in video editing, provide suggestions for video optimization, and offer feedback.

Target users: TikTokers, Video Editors

Revenue model: Monthly subscription fee, Commission-based model

Marketing Ideas: Email marketing, social media campaigns, and referral programs.

100 ChatPromotion: AI-powered Chatbot for TikTok Promotion

Alternative Names:

- ChatPromotion
- ChatBoost
- ChatGrow

Tagline:

"Promote your TikTok account with ChatPromotion AI chatbot"

ChatPromotion is a micro SaaS platform that helps TikTokers to promote their accounts with an AI-powered chatbot. With ChatPromotion, you can easily create custom chatbots that can manage your social media accounts, provide personalized promotion suggestions, and offer analytics.

Target users: TikTokers, Digital Marketers

Revenue model: Monthly subscription fee, Commission-based model

Marketing Ideas: Email marketing, social media campaigns, and referral programs.

101 ChatHashtags:
Chatbot for TikTok Hashtags

Alternative Names:

- ChatHashtags
- ChatTag
- ChatTrend

Tagline:

"Use better hashtags with ChatHashtags AI chatbot"

ChatHashtags is a micro SaaS platform that helps TikTokers to use better hashtags with an AI-powered chatbot. With ChatHashtags, you can easily create custom chatbots that can assist in hashtag research, provide suggestions for trending hashtags, and offer analytics.

Target users: TikTokers, Social Media Managers

Revenue model: Monthly subscription fee, Commission-based model

Marketing Ideas: Email marketing, social media campaigns, and referral programs.

102 ChatEngage:
Chatbot for TikTok Engagement

Alternative Names:

- ChatEngage
- ChatAudience
- ChatConnect

Tagline:

"Engage better with your TikTok audience with ChatEngage AI chatbot"

ChatEngage is a micro SaaS platform that helps TikTokers to engage better with their audience with an AI-powered chatbot. With ChatEngage, you can easily create custom chatbots that can manage your social media accounts, provide personalized content suggestions, and offer audience analytics.

Target users: TikTokers, Social Media Managers

Revenue model: Monthly subscription fee, Commission-based model

Marketing Ideas: Email marketing, social media campaigns, and referral programs.

103 ChatAnalytics: AI-powered Chatbot for TikTok Analytics

Alternative Names:

- ChatAnalytics
- ChatMetrics
- ChatTrack

Tagline:

"Track your TikTok progress with ChatAnalytics AI chatbot"

ChatAnalytics is a micro SaaS platform that helps TikTokers to track their progress with an AI-powered chatbot. With ChatAnalytics, you can easily create custom chatbots that can provide personalized analytics, monitor TikTok progress, and offer insights.

Target users: TikTokers, Digital Marketers

Revenue model: Monthly subscription fee, Freemium model

Marketing Ideas: Influencer marketing, content marketing, and social media campaigns.

104 ChatHashtags: AI-powered Chatbot for Instagram Hashtags

Alternative Names:

- ChatHashtags
- ChatTag
- ChatTrend

Tagline:

"Use better hashtags with ChatHashtags AI chatbot"

ChatHashtags is a micro SaaS platform that helps Instagram Influencers to use better hashtags with an AI-powered chatbot. With ChatHashtags, you can easily create custom chatbots that can assist in hashtag research, provide suggestions for trending hashtags, and offer analytics.

Target users: Instagram Influencers, Social Media Managers

Revenue model: Monthly subscription fee, Commission-based model

Marketing Ideas: Email marketing, social media campaigns, and referral programs.

105 ChatEngage: AI-powered Chatbot for Instagram Engagement

Alternative Names:

- ChatEngage
- ChatAudience
- ChatConnect

Tagline:

"Engage better with your Instagram audience with ChatEngage AI chatbot"

ChatEngage is a micro SaaS platform that helps Instagram Influencers to engage better with their audience with an AI-powered chatbot. With ChatEngage, you can easily create custom chatbots that can manage your social media accounts, provide personalized content suggestions, and offer audience analytics.

Target users: Instagram Influencers, Social Media Managers

Revenue model: Monthly subscription fee, Commission-based model

Marketing Ideas: Email marketing, social media campaigns, and referral programs.

106 ChatPromotion: AI-powered Chatbot for Instagram Promotion

Alternative Names:

- ChatPromotion
- ChatBoost
- ChatGrow

Tagline:

"Promote your Instagram account with ChatPromotion AI chatbot"

ChatPromotion is a micro SaaS platform that helps Instagram Influencers to promote their accounts with an AI-powered chatbot. With ChatPromotion, you can easily create custom chatbots that can manage your social media accounts, provide personalized promotion suggestions, and offer analytics.

Target users: Instagram Influencers, Digital Marketers

Revenue model: Monthly subscription fee, Commission-based model

Marketing Ideas: Email marketing, social media campaigns, and referral programs.

107 ChatAnalytics: Chatbot for Instagram Analytics

Alternative Names:

- ChatAnalytics
- ChatMetrics
- ChatTrack

Tagline:

"Track your Instagram progress with ChatAnalytics AI chatbot"

ChatAnalytics is a micro SaaS platform that helps Instagram Influencers to track their progress with an AI-powered chatbot. With ChatAnalytics, you can easily create custom chatbots that can provide personalized analytics, monitor Instagram progress, and offer insights.

Target users: Instagram Influencers, Digital Marketers

Revenue model: Monthly subscription fee, Freemium model

Marketing Ideas: Influencer marketing, content marketing, and social media campaigns.

108 ChatContent:
Chatbot for Instagram Content Creation

Alternative Names:

- ChatContent
- ChatCreate
- ChatPost

Tagline:

"Create better Instagram content with ChatContent AI chatbot"

ChatContent is a micro SaaS platform that helps Instagram Influencers to create better content with an AI-powered chatbot. With ChatContent, you can easily create custom chatbots that can assist in content creation, provide suggestions for post optimization, and offer feedback.

Target users: Instagram Influencers, Content Creators

Revenue model: Monthly subscription fee, Commission-based model

Marketing Ideas: Email marketing, social media campaigns, and referral programs.

109 ChatHashtags: AI-powered Chatbot for Twitter Hashtags

Alternative Names:

- ChatHashtags
- ChatTag
- ChatTrend

Tagline:

"Use better hashtags with ChatHashtags AI chatbot"

ChatHashtags is a micro SaaS platform that helps Twitter users to use better hashtags with an AI-powered chatbot. With ChatHashtags, you can easily create custom chatbots that can assist in hashtag research, provide suggestions for trending hashtags, and offer analytics.

Target users: Twitter users, Social Media Managers

Revenue model: Monthly subscription fee, Commission-based model

Marketing Ideas: Email marketing, social media campaigns, and referral programs.

110 ChatEngage: Chatbot for Twitter Engagement

Alternative Names:

- ChatEngage
- ChatAudience
- ChatConnect

Tagline:

"Engage better with your Twitter audience with ChatEngage AI chatbot"

ChatEngage is a micro SaaS platform that helps Twitter users to engage better with their audience with an AI-powered chatbot. With ChatEngage, you can easily create custom chatbots that can manage your social media accounts, provide personalized content suggestions, and offer audience analytics.

Target users: Twitter users, Social Media Managers

Revenue model: Monthly subscription fee, Commission-based model

Marketing Ideas: Email marketing, social media campaigns, and referral programs.

111 ChatPromotion: AI-powered Chatbot for Twitter Promotion

Alternative Names:

- ChatPromotion
- ChatBoost
- ChatGrow

Tagline:

"Promote your Twitter account with ChatPromotion AI chatbot"

ChatPromotion is a micro SaaS platform that helps Twitter users to promote their accounts with an AI-powered chatbot. With ChatPromotion, you can easily create custom chatbots that can manage your social media accounts, provide personalized promotion suggestions, and offer analytics.

Target users: Twitter users, Digital Marketers

Revenue model: Monthly subscription fee, Commission-based model

Marketing Ideas: Email marketing, social media campaigns, and referral programs.

112 ChatAnalytics: Chatbot for Twitter Analytics

Alternative Names:

- ChatAnalytics
- ChatMetrics
- ChatTrack

Tagline:

"Track your Twitter progress with ChatAnalytics AI chatbot"

ChatAnalytics is a micro SaaS platform that helps Twitter users to track their progress with an AI-powered chatbot. With ChatAnalytics, you can easily create custom chatbots that can provide personalized analytics, monitor Twitter progress, and offer insights.

Target users: Twitter users, Digital Marketers

Revenue model: Monthly subscription fee, Freemium model

Marketing Ideas: Influencer marketing, content marketing, and social media campaigns.

113 ChatContent:
Chatbot for Twitter Content Creation

Alternative Names:

- ChatContent
- ChatCreate
- ChatPost

Tagline:

"Create better Twitter content with ChatContent AI chatbot"

ChatContent is a micro SaaS platform that helps Twitter users to create better content with an AI-powered chatbot. With ChatContent, you can easily create custom chatbots that can assist in content creation, provide suggestions for post optimization, and offer feedback.

Target users: Twitter users, Content Creators

Revenue model: Monthly subscription fee, Commission-based model

Marketing Ideas: Email marketing, social media campaigns, and referral programs.

Chapter 9:
The Power of No Code

Starting a Micro SaaS business can seem daunting, especially if you don't have coding experience. But with the rise of No-Code platforms, it's easier than ever to turn your idea into a fully functioning product without writing a single line of code.

> *No Code platforms are designed to be user-friendly, and intuitive, and require little to no technical knowledge. They offer a variety of features and tools that allow you to create everything from websites to mobile apps to custom software solutions.*

In this report, we want to provide you with a rolodex of ten No Code platforms to help you bring your Micro SaaS business to life. These platforms offer different levels of complexity and functionality, so you can choose the one that best fits your needs and skill level.

The beauty of No Code is that it allows you to rapidly build and get to market faster, without hiring coders or expensive and often unreliable freelance coders. With these platforms, you can focus on what you do best: identifying a market need, developing a unique value proposition, establishing a pricing strategy, and creating a marketing plan.

So whether you're a seasoned entrepreneur or just starting out, No Code platforms can help you bring your ideas to life and turn them into successful Micro SaaS businesses. So without further ado, let's explore the power of No Code and the platforms that can help you make it happen.

Bubble

(https://bubble.io/):

A platform for building web and mobile apps without code. Bubble allows you to design your app using a drag-and-drop interface and customize it using workflows and plugins.

Airtable

(https://airtable.com/):

A cloud-based spreadsheet and database management platform that lets you organize data, collaborate with team members, and build custom apps without any coding skills.

Zapier

(https://zapier.com/):

A tool that helps you automate workflows by connecting different web applications together. Zapier allows you to create workflows or "Zaps" by using triggers and actions from different apps.

Webflow

(https://webflow.com/):

A platform that allows you to design, build, and launch custom websites without any coding. Webflow offers a drag-and-drop interface, customizable templates, and integrations with popular tools like Mailchimp and Google Analytics.

Glide

(https://www.glideapps.com/):

A platform for building mobile apps without code. Glide lets you create apps by designing a Google Sheet, which is then automatically turned into a mobile app that can be shared with others.

Adalo

(https://www.adalo.com/):

A platform for building mobile apps without code. Adalo offers a drag-and-drop interface, pre-built components, and integrations with popular tools like Stripe and Zapier.

Carrd

(https://carrd.co/):

A platform for building landing pages and simple websites without any coding. Carrd offers a range of templates, a drag-and-drop interface, and custom domain support.

AppSheet

(https://www.appsheet.com/):

A platform for building mobile and web apps without code. AppSheet allows you to design your app using a spreadsheet and customize it using a drag-and-drop interface.

Notion

(https://www.notion.so/):

A productivity and project management tool that allows you to create custom pages, databases, and workflows without any coding. Notion also offers integrations with popular tools like Slack and Trello.

And to close up here's the platform to bring it all together:

ProductDyno

(https://www.productdyno.com)

ProductDyno is a powerful, API-based platform that offers a wide range of benefits for Micro SaaS builders of all kinds, especially those building chatbot tools and other commercial digital products.

One of the main benefits of ProductDyno is its cost-effectiveness. By leveraging its APIs, developers can save both time and money when building their own micro SaaS platform. The APIs handle essential features such as user management, payment integrations, licensing, and more, freeing up time and resources for focusing on the core functionalities of your product.

ProductDyno also comes with a built-in affiliate system that can help grow your user base and increase customer acquisition. The system is viral, which means that users can easily refer their friends and family, earning rewards in the process. This is an excellent way to incentivize your users to promote your product and generate more business for you.

Another great benefit of ProductDyno is its integration capabilities. It comes with over 30 native integrations, as well as over 2,000 additional integrations, making it easy to connect with other tools and platforms that you may already be using (for instance Zapier). This ensures that all of your tools are working together seamlessly, streamlining your workflow and making it easier to manage your business.

In addition, ProductDyno has a fantastic integrated shopping cart that supports one-time payments and recurring subscriptions and you can also connect to third party platforms too.

The "Collections" feature is perfect for offering upsell and upgrade plans to increase your profits and customer value. This feature allows you to create customized upgrade paths and offers that cater to your users' unique needs and preferences.

NOTES

_____

_____

_____

_____

_____

_____

_____

_____

_____

_____

_____

_____

_____

_____

_____

_____

_____

_____

_____

_____

NOTES

_____

_____

_____

_____

_____

_____

_____

_____

_____

_____

_____

_____

_____

_____

_____

_____

_____

_____

NOTES

NOTES